YELLOWSTONE
impressions

photography by Fred Pflughoft

FARCOUNTRY
PRESS

Above: Sunrise over Yellowstone Lake from Gull Point.

Facing page: Quaking aspen is the world's largest single organism in total biomass.

Title page: The major thermal features in Yellowstone National Park are found along the Firehole River.

Front cover: Algae started growing in Morning Glory Pool after visitors threw rocks, coins, and garbage in the pool, partially clogging its vent and cooling it.

Back cover: Yellowstone Falls.

Photographs by John L. Hinderman appear on pages 6, 12, 35, 44, 45, 49, 67

ISBN 1-56037-209-5
Photographs © by Fred Pflughoft except as noted above
© 2002 Farcountry Press

Created, produced, and designed in the United States. Printed in Korea.

Above: A combination of mineral oxides and algae colors the rock along Palette Spring.

Left: West Thumb Geyser Basin was formed by a large volcanic explosion around 150,000 years ago. The basin later filled with water, creating an extension to Yellowstone Lake.

Above: Elk are a common sight during winter in the outlying towns around Yellowstone.

Facing page: An American white pelican, one of North America's largest birds, seen from Fishing Bridge on the Yellowstone River.

Above: Lewis's monkeyflowers occur only in wet places, usually at elevations between 5,000 and 10,000 feet. They occasionally are eaten by mountain sheep, elk, and deer.

Right: When the soil is disturbed, either through forest fire or cultivation, fireweed invades and helps heal the scar. Fireweed also is a valuable range forage plant, a favorite of grizzly bears.

Above: The Grand Canyon of the Yellowstone River was formed by erosion rather than glaciation.

Facing page: At Canary Springs, hot water ascends through ancient limestone deposits instead of the silica-rich lava flows of more common hot springs.

Above: Some grizzly bears are radio-collared, then tracked in Yellowstone National Park in order to help biologists understand how people can best coexist with them.

Right: Lupine's purple ornaments a park valley.

Following pages: American bison feeding near Lower Geyser Basin in late spring. Most of their diet consists of grasses, sedges, and forbs.

Above: Most of the yellows in the rock of the Grand Canyon are a result of the presence of iron.

Right: Orange Spring Mound at Mammoth Hot Springs.

Above: Bunsen Peak and a dried pond bottom.

Left: Storm Point on Yellowstone Lake is aptly named. The currents, combined with strong southwest winds, can create waves as high as five or six feet on the lake.

Right: Pelican Creek marshlands are part of the invaluable wetlands found in the Greater Yellowstone Ecosystem.

Below: Kepler Cascades are some of the loveliest falls in Yellowstone.

Left: The leaves of quaking aspen, the most widely distributed tree in North America, tremble in the lightest breeze. The sound is especially melodious in the fall as the leaves dry out.

Below: Groundsel grows in a burned area near Midway Geyser Basin.

Above: Bull elk form breeding harems to a greater degree than most other deer.

Right: The highly-eroded Grand Canyon of the Yellowstone was probably the result of faulting, which allowed accelerated erosion. Tower Fall trail is a popular place to view the canyon.

Right: The shoreline of Yellowstone Lake as seen from West Thumb Geyser Basin. Geysers, hot springs, and deep canyons make up the bottom of the lake.

Below: Old Faithful is neither the biggest nor most regular geyser in the park, but it is the most watched.

Above: With recent changes in fishing regulations, fish populations have rebounded. Most of the park's Yellowstone cutthroat trout are in Yellowstone Lake.

Right: The Gibbon River has fairly long stretches of quiet water; it originates at Grebe Lake in the heart of the Solfatara Plateau.

Above: Moose Falls on Crawfish Creek during heavy runoff.

Left: The Lewis River Canyon in early summer.

Right: The canyon below Lower Falls was once the site of a geyser basin, probably around the time of the last glaciation.

Below: Along Yellowstone Lake.

Left: West Thumb Geyser Basin consists of a strip of geysers, hot springs, and a few mud pots.

Below: Castle Geyser may be as old as 5,000 to 15,000 years, evidenced by its enormous cone.

Right: The Gardner River is best known by local people for its thermally heated swimming hole near the north entrance.

Below: The road leading from the East Entrance follows the North Fork of the Shoshone River, then leads directly to Yellowstone Lake and the Fishing Bridge.

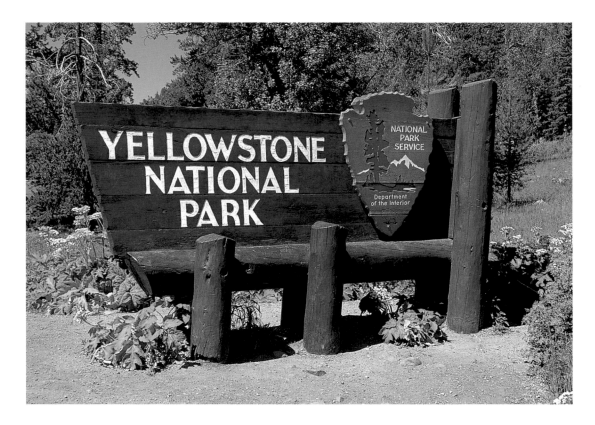

Above: The boardwalk allows visitors a closeup of Beehive Geyser as steam is forced out of its vent. Its eruption duration is about five minutes.

Facing page: Marble Terrace at Mammoth Hot Springs is a fine illustration of the travertine formations in the area.

Above: Young Hopeful Geyser is a collection of small vents; the two largest combine to form a column between two and six feet tall.

Right: Great Fountain Geyser sits in the middle of a pretty sinter formation.

Above: Lily pads and blossoms adorn Isa Lake.

Facing page: Rose Creek runs through the Lamar Buffalo Ranch, which was built in the early 20th century to increase the herd size of the remaining bison in Yellowstone. Yellowstone was the last refuge of wild bison in the United States at the end of the 19th century.

Right: In winter, plumes of steam add to Mammoth Terrace's already stunning sight.

Below: Gibbon Falls.

Above: After a gestation of nine to ten months, a cow bison typically gives birth to a single calf weighing about forty pounds.

Right: When Excelsior Geyser was active in the 1880s, its eruptions reached 300 feet tall and 300 feet wide, greatly increasing the volume of the Firehole River for a half hour after each eruption.

Above: Mount Washburn reaches 10,243 feet. The panorama from its summit takes in the entire park.

Above: With the gray wolf's return to Yellowstone National Park, many believe the predator-prey ratio is more in balance.

Right: New thermal activities may create skeletons of once-living trees.

Below: Great Fountain Geyser is known for its superbursts—burst of water over 150 feet—and its blue bubbles—large expanding steam bubbles.

Above: The Firehole River is named for the steam witnessed by early trappers in the area. Trappers called a mountain valley a hole, thus the name.

Facing page: Nez Perce Creek provides river habitat for fish, reptiles, birds, and mammals.

Above: There are more geysers in Yellowstone than anywhere else on earth; Shell Geyser in the Biscuit Basin is among them.

Facing page: Thomas Moran's early painting of Tower Falls played an important role in the establishment of Yellowstone National Park in 1872.

Above: Railings of lodgepole pine contribute to the beauty of the lobby of the Old Faithful Inn, built during the winter of 1903-04. Lodgepole pines cover nearly two-thirds of the land in Yellowstone.

Facing page: Castle Geyser, a cone-type geyser, has intervals of nine to eleven hours and blasts steam sixty to ninety feet high.

Above: Glacier lilies grow in subalpine meadows, their bright yellow flowers appearing as snowfields disappear.

Facing page: The Yellowstone River cuts through the Hayden Valley in lazy arcs. Grizzly bears may be spotted in the Hayden Valley and Central Plateau region.

Above: Paintbrush is a common perennial herb that is a favorite among admirers of wildflowers.

Right: Bold-colored underbrush near Elk Creek.

Left: American bison grazing along Soda Butte Creek in the Lamar Valley. Their range historically extended from the southern Yukon to northern Mexico and east to the Appalachian Mountains.

Above: Seismograph Spring and Bluebell Pool are found in the West Thumb Geyser Basin.

Right: Thermal basins, such as Bluebell Pool, encourage the early germination of plant life.

Above: The bugle of the bull elk is a much-anticipated sound each fall among Yellowstone's visitors and cow elk.

Left: Sunset over Junction Butte.

Above: A weak carbonic acid solution dissolves great quantities of limestone as it works up through the rock layers. The result is Minerva Terrace.

Right: The Lewis River below Lewis Falls as it heads toward its meeting with the Snake River.

Above: Aspens in the Hoodoos.

Left: Electric Peak and Sepulcher Mountain, above Swan Lake.

Facing page: Aspen can be differentiated from paper birch by its black eyes, which are scars where branches once grew.

Below: Some species, such as beavers, tiger salamanders, and American dippers, are year-round residents of Yellowstone's wetlands.

Above: The Blacktail Deer Plateau is open, high country; a good place to see bison, coyotes, and wolves in winter.

Left: The Gibbon River meandering through Gibbon Meadow provides good habitat for large mammals as well as aquatic insects.

Above: A close look at Midway Geyser Basin's Grand Prismatic Spring.

Right: Looking past The Hoodoos to Bunsen Peak bathed in sunset light.

Above: Yellow-bellied marmots eat, sleep, and doze on rocks after they emerge from their burrows. They are also exceptional sentinels and good housekeepers.

Left: Late in the day at Back Basin in Norris Geyser Basin.

Fred Pflughoft

Fred Pflughoft turned from watercolor painting to landscape photography in 1988. His full-color photography appears regularly in regional and national periodicals, on calendars and postcards from American and Canadian publishers, and is featured in the Farcountry Press books *Wyoming Wild and Beautiful, Oregon Wild and Beautiful, Yellowstone Wild and Beautiful, Grand Teton Wild and Beautiful, Wyoming Impressions,* and *Wyoming's Historic Forts.* He and his wife, Sue, have twin sons who join them in outdoor activities all year around.